T0368363

# What You May Not Know
## About Individuals
# LIVING
# WITH
# AUTISM

MARSHA NIXON POWELL

authorHOUSE®

AuthorHouse™
1663 Liberty Drive
Bloomington, IN 47403
www.authorhouse.com
Phone: 833-262-8899

Published by AuthorHouse  11/07/2024

ISBN: 979-8-8230-3722-8 (sc)
ISBN: 979-8-8230-3721-1 (e)

Library of Congress Control Number: 2024923538

Print information available on the last page.

This book is dedicated to my family and in loving memory of my mother, Betty and my sister, Brenda.

# ACKNOWLEDGMENTS

I would like to give love and appreciation to my daughters: Qiana and Cierra, and my grandson, Mark: for their encouragement, and continued love and support.

# CONTENTS

# CONTENTS

# CHAPTER 1

# WHAT IS AUTISM SPECTRUM DISORDER (ASD)?

**Autism Spectrum Disorder (ASD)** is a condition related to brain development that impacts how a person perceives and socializes with others, causing problems in social interaction and communication. This disorder also includes limited and repetitive patterns of behavior.

Autism spectrum disorder begins in early childhood and eventually causes problems functioning in society – socially, in school and at work. Often children show symptoms of autism within the first year. A small number of children appear to develop normally in the first year, and then go through a period of regression between 18 and 24 months when they develop autism symptoms.

While there is no cure for autism spectrum disorder, intensive, early treatment can make a big difference in the lives of many children.

## Social communication and interaction

A child or adult with autism spectrum disorder may have problems with social and communication skills, including any of these signs:

- Fails to respond to his or her name or appears not to hear you at times
- Resists cuddling and holding, and seems to prefer playing alone, retreating into his or her own world
- Has poor eye contact and lacks facial expressions
- Doesn't speak or has delayed speech
- Doesn't express emotions or feelings and appears unaware of other's feelings
- Has difficulty recognizing nonverbal cues, such as interpreting other people's facial expressions, body positions or tone of voice

## Patterns of Behavior

A child or adult with autism spectrum disorder (ASD) may have limited, repetitive patterns of behavior, interests or activities, including many of these signs:

- Performs repetitive movements, such as rocking, spinning or hand flapping or stemming (repetitive actions, such as jiggling a foot, twirling hair, finger flicking)
- Has a problem with coordination or has odd movement patterns, such as clumsiness or walking on toes, and has odd, stiff or exaggerated body language

- Is unusually sensitive to light, sound or touch, yet may be indifferent to pain or temperature
- Doesn't engage in imitative or make-believe play
- Fixates on an object or activity with abnormal intensity or focus
- Has specific food preferences, such as eating only a few foods, or refusing foods with a certain texture
- Inappropriate or sudden laughter is a common symptom of autism spectrum disorder (ASD). It can happen frequently and at unexpected times.

While laughter is normal, excessive or inappropriate laughter can be disruptive. Understanding can help with responding with empathy rather than frustration. By being patient and supportive, we can better assist autistic individuals in navigating their unique emotional experiences.

According to a report by the National Health Service (NHS), "being autistic does not mean you have an illness or disease. It means your brain works in a different way from other people."

## How is ASD Diagnosed?

Each child with autism spectrum disorder (ASD) is different. There is no one test that will diagnose a child, and there is no one sign that all children exhibit. ASD is a neurodevelopment condition. It occurs in the brain. There may be components to it, but the exact causes are unknown.

Signs of autism can manifest in babies as young as 12 months. They can include avoiding eye contact, and other children may have delayed language skills, or they may give unrelated answers when they are asked questions. A child may struggle to show or discuss their feelings. They may not understand how other people are feeling. They may not respond to facial expressions or verbal cues. Many people with ASD become upset when their routines change. They may organize themselves or mandate routines, which others find unwarranted.

Doctors can diagnose a child with ASD when they are as young as 18 months. Spotting the signs of ASD on someone is one step for diagnosis. Another step for determining, is assessing when a child began walking or talking can determine ASD signs when children diagnosed learn to talk late. Doctors can conduct evaluations to screen for autism. Doctors examine medical records and run tests with the children themselves. After a few visits, they can determine what is going on with the child.

Because autism spectrum disorder varies widely in symptoms and severity, making a diagnosis may be difficult. There isn't a specific medical test to determine the disorder. Instead, a specialist may:

- Observe your child and ask how your child's social interactions, communication skills and behavior have developed and changed over time
- Give your child tests covering hearing, speech, language, and behavioral issues
- Include other specialists in determining a diagnosis

## Living With Autism

If you are diagnosed with autism, you'll have it your entire life, but early treatment can make a big difference for a child with autism. If you think your child shows symptoms of ASD, tell your doctor as soon as possible.

---------------------- CHAPTER 2 ----------------------

# SIGNS AND SYMPTOMS
# OF AUTISM

People with Autism Spectrum Disorder (ASD) often have
problems with social communication and interaction, and
restricted or repetitive behaviors or interests. People with
ASD may also have different ways of learning, moving or
paying attention. These characteristics can make life very
challenging. It is important to note that some people without
ASD might also have some of these symptoms.

## Risk Factors

There is not just one cause of ASD. Many different factors
have been identified that may make a child more likely to
have ASD, including environmental, biologic, and genetic
factors.

Although we know little about specific causes, the available evidence suggests that the following may put children at greater risk for developing ASD:

- Have a sibling with ASD
- Have certain genetic or chromosomal conditions, such as fragile X syndrome (FXS) – is a genetic disorder and one of the most common causes of inherited intellectual disability, or tuberous sclerosis – is an uncommon genetic disorder that causes tumors to develop in many parts of the body. These tumors are not cancer.
- Experiencing complications at birth
- Being born to older parents

## Signs and Symptoms of Autism in an Adult

Autism symptoms in adults tend to be most prominent in communication skills, interests, emotional and behavioral patterns, have sensitivity to stimuli, such as noise and touch.

Listed are some common signs and characteristics:

1. Social challenges:

   - Difficulty understanding others.
   - Anxiety in social situations.
   - Bluntness or rudeness in communication.
   - Trouble interpreting non-verbal cues (e.g., eye-rolling, facial expressions).

2. Cognitive Differences:

   - Literal thinking.
   - Difficulty understanding phrases or sarcasm.
   - Challenges with theory of mind (seeing things from another's perspective).

3. Behavioral Patterns:

   - Need for routine
   - Special interests or hobbies
   - Careful planning

4. Sensory Sensitivity:

   - Heightened sensitivity to sensory stimuli (e.g., lights, sounds, textures).
   - Masking or camouflaging (hiding automatic traits).
   - Intense anxiety of changes in daily routine.

Not all adults exhibit the same symptoms, and some may develop coping mechanisms that mask their diagnosis. If autism is suspected, seeking professional evaluation is essential for accurate diagnosis and support.

# CHAPTER 3

# WHAT TO DO AFTER AN ASD DIAGNOSIS

Autism appears to be everywhere. One in 54 American children have autism spectrum disorder (ASD). It cuts across all demographic groups, and children show a wide range of symptoms. Obtaining an autism diagnosis is essential to getting your child started on their therapies. Some parents don't know what to do after they receive a diagnosis, so they don't bother with getting one.

As they mature, some children with autism spectrum disorder (ASD) become more engaged with others and show fewer disturbances in behavior from, becoming less severe with problems, eventually may lead normal or near-normal lives. Others, however, continue to have difficulty with language or social skills, and the teen years can bring worse behavioral and emotional problems.

After an ASD diagnosis consider the following steps:

1. Educate yourself about the diagnosis.
2. Adjust the child's own environment to better meet their needs.
3. Seek professional therapeutic services, including occupational and physical therapy, speech therapy, behavioral and emotional therapy, and social skill-building groups.
4. Create a sensory-friendly environment.
5. Implement a routine.

## The Dos and Don'ts After an Autism Diagnosis

It's true that some people unfamiliar with autism might stop coming around after the diagnosis. They do not understand the behaviors, the meltdowns, the necessity for routine, or the jargon that is used. If you find yourself in need of understanding, find a parent who has already walked a few miles in your shoes.

## Adults Diagnosed with Autism

Receiving an autism diagnosis as an adult can be a life-changing experience that brings a mix of emotions and challenges. For many, it may provide a sense of relief and validation, finally offering an exchange for the struggles and differences they have experienced throughout their lives.

However, the journey of self-discovery and navigating as a newly diagnosed autistic adult can also be overwhelming and confusing.

## What To Do After a Child's Autism Diagnosis

It is easy to become overwhelmed after you receive your child's autism diagnosis. It is important that you educate yourself on autism spectrum disorder (ASD) and learn how to best help your child and yourself. By listening to your child, you can create a structured environment and build stability in your home. Make sure you have help by engaging family members and friends with your situation.

## Some Celebrities on the spectrum include:

- Bruce Willis' daughter, Tallulah Belle, shared that she was diagnosed with autism in her 30's.
- Susan Boyle, Britain's Got Talent star, was diagnosed at 51, with Asperger's Syndrome, which is a form of autism.
- Sir Anthony Hopkins, was diagnosed with Asperger's in his 70s
- Elon Musk, is the world's richest person, CEO & Chief Engineer at SpaceX; CEO & Product Architect of Telsa, revealed he had Asperger's syndrome on Saturday Night Live in 2021

# CHAPTER 4

# THE MYTHS AND FACTS ABOUT AUTISM

## Nine Myths About Autism

- Eighty years ago, autism was thought to affect only one in 2,500 – yet today one in 36 children are believed to have autism spectrum disorder (ASD).
- Vaccines do not cause autism. Some people have had concerns that ASD might be linked to the vaccines children receive, but studies have shown that there is no link between receiving vaccines and developing autism spectrum disorder (ASD).
- Autism only affects boys. It is true that many more boys than girls are diagnosed younger and more frequently, but that is often because girls may exhibit different social and communication problems.
- "Autistic people lack empathy and may have difficulty interpreting non-verbal cues and body language", says Professor Francesca Happe, a professor of cognitive neuroscience at King's College

in London. "But most autistic people have lots of emotional empathy."

- Autistic people aren't sociable. Although some social interactions can be puzzling for autistic people, many are very sociable, and can be autistic and an extrovert.

- Autistic people lack emotions. They might have different ways of expressing emotions, but it's certainly not true that they're lacking emotions.

- Autism can be cured. Autism is now recognized as a different, not deficient, neurotype, which doesn't need to be cured and should be respected.

- Autistic people are violent. "While some people with autism may exhibit challenging behaviors, it's usually an attempt to communicate or escape an overwhelming situation", explains Professor Happe. More children may suffer "tantrums" due to frustrations, not necessarily violent behaviors.

- Autism only affects children. Most autistic people are adults and autism a lifelong condition. One of the benefits of being diagnosed, especially as a late diagnosis, is it allows a person who has been self-critical for many years to be more self-compassionate.

## 10 Facts About Autism

1. Autism spectrum disorder affects one in 36 children.
2. Boys are nearly five times more likely than girls to be diagnosed with ASD.
3. ASD is one of the fastest-growing developmental disorders in the United States.

4. ASD affects all nationalities, all creeds, all religions, all races and both sexes.

5. Autism spectrum disorder is a developmental disability (ASD) that often presents with challenges before the age of three and lasts throughout a person's lifetime.

6. Supporting an individual with ASD costs a family $60,000 a year on average. The cost of lifelong care to be reduced by 2/3 with early diagnosis and intervention.

7. Each person with autism spectrum disorder (ASD) is a unique individual; people with ASD differ as much from one another as to all people.

8. An individual with autism spectrum disorder (ASD) may be very creative and find a passion and talent for music, theater, dance, and singing quite easily with autism.

9. There is no federal requirement for providing support services to people with autism in adulthood. This leaves many navigating these types of services on their own.

10. Many people with autism spectrum disorder (ASD) are successfully living and working and contributing to the well-being, are in their local communities. This is most likely to happen when appropriate services are delivered during the child's education years.

# CHAPTER 5

# NONVERBAL ASD HIGH-FUNCTIONING VS. LOW-FUNCTIONING AUTISM

Nonverbal autism is a term used for a subgroup of people with autism spectrum disorder (ASD) who never learn to speak more than a few words. An estimated 25% to 35% of autistic children are considered nonverbal. Nonverbal autism tends to occur in people with high support needs, or what is known as level 3 autism. The difficulty in developing language skills and understanding what others say to them. They also often have difficulty communicating nonverbally, such as through hand gestures, eye contact, and facial expressions.

# Understanding Nonspeaking (Nonverbal) Autism

Autism Spectrum Disorder (ASD) is an umbrella term used to identify a variety of neurodevelopmental disorder. These disorders are grouped together because they have similar effect on a person's ability to:

- Communicate
- Socialize
- Behave
- Develop

Nonspeaking or nonverbal autism refers to cases in which an autistic person has a delay or difficulty with speech which can range from mild to severe. Some people do not speak at all. Even if an autistic person is non-speaking, they may still use words – or other ways (such as in writing). They may also understand the words that are spoken to them or that they overhear.

# Can a Non-verbal autistic child develop the ability to speak?

There is hope for language development and communication skills.

1.  Early Intervention. Timely intervention is crucial. Some nonspeaking autistic people eventually begin to talk, especially with early support.

2. Speech Development. Research shows that language development can occur from up to age 13. Some non-speaking children become fluent speakers after age 4, and many start using phrases also sign language.

Each individual is unique, and outcomes vary. Patience, understanding, and tailored approaches are essential.

Here are some ways to help:

1. Communication Alternatives:

   • Augmentative and Alternative Communication (AAC): Explore AAC methods like sign language, picture boards, or communication opportunities
   • Visual supports: Use visual cues by patterning symbols to aid communication.

2. Sensory support:

   • Understand sensory sensitivities and provide a calm, predictable environment.
   • Offer sensory-friendly tools (weighted blankets, fidget toys).

3. Social interaction:

   • Encourage social play and interaction
   • Model communication by directing to them and waiting for responses

4. Speech Therapy:

- Consult a speech therapist for tailored exercises.
- Focus on oral motor skills and imitation.

5. Individualized Education Plan (IEP):

- Collaborate with educators to create an IEP Plan

Just because someone is nonverbal, doesn't mean they can't hear or understand what's being said.

> **"Being nonverbal does not mean I want you to be my voice. It means I need your help in finding ways to express mine."**
>
> JOY OF AUTISM

# High-Functioning vs. Low-Functioning Autism

Autism is a spectrum disorder, and people with autism can be classified as high-functioning or low-functioning. High-functioning autism (HFA) refers to autistic people who can generally function well in society, often through masking their autistic behaviors from others by copying "normal" behaviors. Individuals with high-functioning autism have average or above-average intelligence and language skills. Low-functioning autism (LFA) have significant intellectual and developmental disabilities. However, regardless of the autism level, the person's need for support can vary for many reasons and may be inconsistent from one day to the next.

## Summary

The terms high-functioning and low-functioning are outdated phrases that can be misleading. Perhaps the most important reason to not use functioning labels is actually autistic adults say these labels are misleading and harmful, and increase the stigma and misperceptions of autism.

> *"The difference between high-functioning and low-functioning is that high-functioning means your deficits are ignored, and low-functioning means your assets are ignored."*
>
> - LAURA TISONICK (FROM CIRCLE OF MOMS BLOG

# CHAPTER 6

# CRITICAL DIFFERENCES IN THE BRAINS OF GIRLS DIAGNOSED WITH AUTISM

Girls have different patterns of connectivity than boys in several brain centers, including motor, language, and visuospatial attention symptoms.

In children with autism, gender differences were observed in the motor cortex, supplementary motor areas, and a portion of the cerebellum, which affect motor function and planning of motor activity.

## More Boys with High-functioning Autism

Among children diagnosed with high-functioning form of autism, boys out-number girls by four to one. Scientists were interested in comparing the experiences of core factors of the disorder between sexes because they have long suspected girls with autism may display symptoms differently, causing them to be underdiagnosed or make it harder for them to get the most appropriate treatment. The brain-scan analysis revealed gender differences in brain structure between typically developing boys and girls.

## Why Girls with Autism Are Diagnosed Later Than Boys

A new study looking at gender differences among children with autism spectrum disorder show that girls have different, less obvious symptoms compared to boys, which could be why they are generally diagnosed later.

Research has found that in general, girls were diagnosed with ASD later than boys. Researchers say their findings suggested that the symptom differences may not lead to early diagnosis in girls, but potentially missed diagnoses altogether.

Understanding the various ways children with ASD present may lead to a better understanding of the disorders.

## Signs and Symptoms of Autism Traits in Girls

- Rely on other children to guide and speak for them
- Depression, anxiety, low frustration levels, or other mental health symptoms
- Different behaviors at home and school

- Has passionate but limited interests
- Hard to make friends

Unfortunately, it is true that autism traits in girls and women are not always the same as those identified in boys and men. This means that females may not get an autism diagnosis until more later in life – if ever.

# CHAPTER 7

# PROVIDING SUPPORT TO YOUR CHILD

## There are six things you can do to support children on the autism spectrum:

1.  Provide a safe space to talk and be sensitive to sensory stimulation.
2.  Help them find their passions. Finding their passions is a crucial step in helping autistic children feel more included.
3.  Help them build confidence. Encourage your child to talk about any problems they may be experiencing. This will enable them to receive the support they require to deal with any issues and support confidence building.
4.  Set formal attainable goals. Setting small, doable goals with your child can be beneficial regardless of where they are on the autism spectrum by talking to them and learning what they want to accomplish. You can set manageable goals that are important to

their lives. Setting goals together with your child can foster a more cooperative relationship that will enable you to provide better support for them.

5.  Help them develop social skills. Each child needs social skills, but children with autism spectrum disorder need them even more.

Some of the most effective ways to support your child's social skills development include:

- Providing structured activities that encourage social interaction: It is easier for kids to learn social skills when they have opportunities to interact with one another.
- Being inclusive: Make sure your child participates in activities with their friends. They will feel more included and assured in their capacity to interact with others.
- Creating limits: Setting boundaries is equally important as ensuring your child participates in social actions.

6.  Don't be afraid to set boundaries. Setting boundaries and helping your child fit in with their peers are both critical.

Here are some tips for setting boundaries with your autistic child:

- Ensure that you are involving your child in appropriate activities. Avoid forcing your child into social situations for which they are not prepared.

- Remain composed when setting boundaries. This will keep your child calm and make it simpler for them to pay attention to you.

## What support do autistic children need?

Autistic children need personalized support tailored to their unique sensory, communication, and social needs, including structured routines and clear expectations.

## Do you need support services if your child is autistic?

No two autistic people are alike. If your child is autistic, you may consider support services, as desired or needed to address any needs your child may have.

## Animals can also help provide support for children with autism

Animals can help autistic children in various ways that can build social communication skills, manage emotions, and build play skills. Some popular pets for autistic children include:

- Cats: They can provide unconditional love and calm companionship.
- Guinea pigs: They are small, fluffy animals. They are naturally friendly and gentle.

- Rabbits: They are safe, adorable companions.
- Fish, domesticated rats, and hamsters.
- Dogs: They are popular therapy animals.

## 10 Best Therapy Dog Breeds for Children with Autism

1. Golden Retriever – they have been used as service and therapy dogs for a long time as they always do their best to please their owners.
2. Beagle – they aren't ideal for all families with autistic individuals, but they are the perfect companion pet for some.
3. Miniature Schnauzer – Despite their small size, they will make an excellent and loyal friend to many adults or children with autism.
4. German Shepard - trained well, they make an amazing and gentle companion to an individual with autism.
5. Bichon Frise – as therapy dogs, they are devoted, happy, and they aren't likely to spook at noises, especially when trained well.
6. Pug – they are a bit more work than some other breeds as they shed a lot, however, they are also quiet compared to other dogs.
7. Samoyed – they are gentle with everyone, and are highly intelligent and easy to train.
8. Corgi – they can be a little tricky to work with as they are highly intelligent, but they make fantastic

    therapy dogs in the right place with the right training.

9. Bernese Mountain Dog – gentle giants are excellent weighted blankets. Can have a calming effect.

10. St. Bernard – take up a lot of space, but are another gentle giant.

## Conclusion

If you need any help or advice when it comes to choosing the right dog breed to help a person with autism, get in contact with professionals at Emotional Support Animal (ESA) Registration.

# CHAPTER 8

# SPECIAL EDUCATION CLASSES/SCHOOLS

## Autism in School: Options, Challenges

There are various educational possibilities for autistic students:

- General education classroom, a resource classroom, a special education classroom, or an autistic-only setting where autistic students thrive in an inclusive class setting, while others are better in more tailored settings. It all depends on the child.
- Many autistic children need some degree of classroom support, but needs vary generally from child to child. Like neurotypical children, some autistic children have more academic challenges than others. Some autistic children will react in ways that do not conform to expectations for traditional classroom settings.

Some examples:

- Running out the classroom and possibly even the building – known as eloping.
- Shutting down and putting their head on the desk or hiding under the desk.
- Have loud, emotional outbursts, such as screaming, crying or sobbing loudly where other students can hear.

## Educational Opportunities for Autistic Children

Some autistic students require special education classes, while others do better with advanced learning opportunities that can then be engaged in the classroom.

Autistic children often qualify for a 504 Plan or Individualized Education Plan (IEP) that allows classroom accommodations. However, just having a medical diagnosis of autism does not automatically qualify a student for accommodations. The district's child study team will determine whether the student requires additional support.

## Special Education

Autistic children are sometimes placed in a special or disability education classroom in their local public school. This option may work well for students with learning disabilities if the teacher is also experienced in teaching autistic children.

## Autism Support Classrooms

Some larger school districts offer autistic support classrooms within their public schools. These classrooms are set up to meet the specific needs of autistic children. They are staffed by teachers and aides trained on both autism and education.

## Private Schools

Private schools may offer similar classes, individualized attention and good resources. This may be a good option for autistic students who excel academically, and are comfortable socializing with neurotypical students with little understanding of autism.

## How To Choose Education Options

Determining the proper placement for autistic learning depends on several factors. Some points to consider as you think about the options are:

- The autistic child's communication abilities and level of social engagement
- Their academic skills
- How they handle interaction with large groups
- Tolerance for sensory input

- Ability to focus in the classroom
- Prior classroom experience

Most autistic children will need extra support in school through a 504 plan or Individualized Education Plan (IEP). This can be a long and sometimes frustrating process. Check with your State Department of Education to find out the rules in your area.

# CHAPTER 9

# LOVE ON THE SPECTRUM

To navigate dating someone on the autism spectrum it is essential to have a basic understanding of autism spectrum disorder (ASD) and its common characteristics. By gaining insight into the unique experiences and perspectives of individuals on the autism spectrum, you can foster a more compassionate and supportive relationship. Often a misconception that individuals on the spectrum want to date others who are on the spectrum. This couldn't be further from the truth. People on the spectrum want to find someone to connect with and can be themselves so don't assume that your partner must be autistic too.

The world of dating and relationships can be tough to navigate, which requires complex, often tedious work to communicate clearly, interpret signals effectively, and understand if your feelings are reciprocated. Because people with autism often have difficulty reading social cues, managing sensory needs, and expressing feelings, that involve dating someone with autism spectrum disorder can be particularly challenging to navigate. But with the right perspective and ability, dually autistic or interabled couples can attain and sustain long-lasting, healthy connections.

Dating as an autistic person has its challenges because it can feel like the stakes for misunderstanding and rejection are high. Autistic people may be a bit more sensitive and specific with their needs, but that doesn't mean they're harder to love – the key is knowing what to pay attention to.

## Dating and Autism – Tips for Success in Love

- Many studies show that autistic adults are less likely to be married, though barriers to diagnose and study limitations make it difficult to determine exact numbers.
- However, when surveyed, many autistic individuals who want to be in romantic relationships report challenges in this area.
- While autistic people can experience challenges in dating and romantic relationships upon communication and understanding of individual unique needs can reduce anxiety around this process. If you are autistic, knowing that you can find a partner who understands and meets your needs helps to improve romance in relationships. If you are not autistic, you can extend compassion to

your partner and help them be comfortable in your relationship.

*"It's okay to say something like, I'm the kind of person who doesn't pick up on hints and flirting. If someone likes me, I hope they will come right out and tell me."*

WENDELIN WHITCOMB AND
MARTHA WASHINGTON - AUTHORS
AND AUTISM ADVOCATES

---------- CHAPTER 10 ----------

# AUTISM SUPPORT GROUPS

Autism support groups are communities of people who share experiences and resources related to autism spectrum disorder.

## Resources and Services for Adults with Autism – Autism Speaks

**Autism Speaks, Inc.** is an American non-profit autism awareness organization and the largest autism research organization in the United States. It sponsors autism research and conducts awareness and outreach activities aimed at families, governments, and the public. It was founded in February, 2005 by Bob Wright and his wife Suzanne, a year after their grandson, Christian, was diagnosed with autism.

**Autism Speaks Walk** is the largest autism fundraising event dedicated to improving the lives of people with autism. Powered by the love of people with autism and the parents, grandparents, siblings, friends, relatives and providers who support them. The funds raised help ensure people of all abilities have access to the tools needed to lead "their best lives".

**Eagles Autism Fund/Challenge** is dedicated to raising funds for innovative research and programs to help unlock the mystery of autism. With the support of incredible participants, The Eagles Autism Challenge has raised over $25 million for autism research and care programs in just six years! The Challenge involves bike riding, running/walking each year at the Lincoln Financial Center in Philadelphia, Pennsylvania.

**Special Olympics Philadelphia** is a bowling tournament held in Philadelphia at Thunderbird Lanes for over 25 years. The yearly tournament is anticipated and looked forward to by more than 125 participants and 100 coaches and volunteers! It's not only about winning, but it is also about making lasting memories with friends, both new and old. During the tournament, a special event is presented, which is a re-enactment of The Olympics Games. Medals and ribbons are awarded to the athletes to encourage fun and competition.

People on the spectrum and their families benefit from autism support groups. Being in a support group for autism can help a person with autism or his/her caregiver:

- Feel less isolated
- Share strategies in dealing with certain situations
- Seek expert advice
- Vent frustrations safely (no judgments)
- Avoid going into depression

## Family Support Groups for Autism

Finding a support group in your location is made easy with a quick google search. Simply type "autism support group" followed by your city or location, which provides a worldwide listing of resources.

## A person with autism is:

Always
Unique
Totally
Intelligent
Sometimes
Mysterious

- ANONYMOUS

---

CHAPTER 11

---

# TRAINING/EMPLOYMENT OPPORTUNITIES FOR ADULTS WITH AUTISM

In most cases, individuals with autism experience delayed launch into the workplace. Those who work typically work low-wage, part-time jobs. Nearly 42% of young adults on the autism spectrum do not work for pay during their early 20s.

## Employment/Training Opportunities for People with Autism include:

1. Technology and computing careers: Tailoring to autistic skills
2. Creative Pursuits: Leveraging unique perspectives in the arts
3. Structures and Detail-oriented Roles: A match for autistic proficiencies

4.  Animal care jobs: The Soothing Effect
5.  Scientific and research positions: Utilizing analytical strategies

Additionally, there are autism-friendly employers in the United States, and organizations that provide career resources and support for individuals with autism.

## Things to Know About Autism and Employment

Most autistic adults are under employed. Approximately half of the autistic adults are employed, but many have part-time jobs or work for which they're overqualified. There are many autistic people working as volunteers or in programs outside the mainstream.

Here are a few key reasons why autistic adults end up in these positions:

- Low expectations: Few schools and sometimes even families expect autistic children to find satisfactory careers. The exception is if they happen to have extra skills. However, the lowered expectations for most autistic children can be destructive to their self-confidence.
- Lack of programs: Most workplace programs for disabled adults were not developed with autism in mind, rather they were maintained to work for people with intellectual or physical disabilities.

- Competition and challenges to getting people in the general community, autistic people have to compete for positions that can be hard for neurodiverse people whose social skills do not match society's norms. These challenges can hamper their performance in job interviews and make it hard for them to engage successfully with co-workers. Some autistic adults also find it hard to manage the physical requirements of the workplace, especially if they have sensitivities to light, sound, and other stimuli that they might not have any control over in these situations.

## Summary

If you're an autistic adult or the parent or caregiver of an autistic person, know that there are a growing number of opportunities for employment. Everyone should be able to have a job that pays them fairly, uses their skills, and gives them a sense of purpose. While autistic adults have a lot to offer employers, there are challenges in the job search process that neurotypical candidates don't face.

To prepare for these challenges, it is important to know what support and resources are available where you live.

## Seven Autism Friendly Employers

- Microsoft – their dedicated Neurodiversity Hiring Program offers job recruitment and career development strategies related to diversity and inclusion

- Ford – they partnered with the Autism Alliance of Michigan to found a program with the specific goal of hiring and supporting autistic employees.
- Ernst and Young – is a huge international accounting firm that has discovered the value of neurodiversity to its bottom line.
- Walgreens – runs a program called REDI, which stands for Retail Employees with Disabilities.
- Home Depot and CVS Caremark - partnered with an organization called Ken's Krew to recruit and train disabled employees.
- AMC Theatre – their FOCUS program, which stands for Furthering Opportunities Cultivating Untapped Strengths, is an employee development program specifically directed toward hiring disabled individuals.

You'll also want to keep an eye on the news to learn about employers who are making a point to develop neurodiversity programs that hire and support autistic workers and other individuals with learning and mental differences.

*"Autism Doesn't Hold People Back at Work. Discrimination Does."*

LUDMILA N. PRASLOVA, PHD,
SHRM-SCP

# ABOUT THE AUTHOR

Marsha Nixon-Powell is a Philadelphia native. She lives with her family in Northeast Philadelphia.

She is a long-time cancer survivor who has been a business owner (Family Day Care) and currently works as a Behavioral Health Technician in the Philadelphia school system with autistic and special-needs students.

Nixon-Powell also works as a home caregiver for senior citizens in the Philadelphia and Bucks County areas. She is an inspiration to those who know her and continues to learn and develop new leadership and professional skills. She is the author of *I'm The Healthiest Sick Person I Know and The Many Rewards and Challenges of Being a Caregiver.*

Printed in the United States
by Baker & Taylor Publisher Services